Ministry to the Sick

GENERAL NOTES

1 **Distinctions in the text** Sections of services with numbers in blue may be omitted. Texts in bold type are to be said by the congregation.

2 **Biblical passages** The sentences, psalms and readings may be read in any duly authorized version.

3 **The Lord's Prayer** On any occasion the Lord's Prayer may be used in its modern form (as in Rite A, see p. 10), or in its modified form (as in Rite B, see p. 16), or in its traditional form (as in the Book of Common Prayer).

Communion with the Sick

NOTES

1 **Preparation** Careful devotional preparation before the service is recommended for every communicant. The form here provided may be used for this purpose.

2 **Communion in Hospital** Where communion takes place in a hospital, the co-operation of the staff should be sought.

3 **Modification** The forms provided may be modified or shortened in the light of pastoral needs, and of the context within which they are used. Other material from Rite A (or Rite B as appropriate) may be used in place of, or in addition to, the forms provided. Whichever order is followed, the greeting, the confession, the absolution, and the Lord's Prayer should always be used. When there is a celebration of the Holy Communion in the presence of the sick, sections 11-14 are always included.

4 **Seasonal Material** Special provision of proper collects, readings, and psalms is made in the order following. The seasonal or Sunday provision may be used in place of that set out here. At Christmas, Easter, and Pentecost some at least of the seasonal provision for the Festival should be used.

5 **Words of Invitation** In the Rite A forms the invitation 'Draw near with faith . . .' is to be used at least on Sundays and other Holy Days, and the invitation 'Jesus is the Lamb of God . . .' may be added. On other days 'Jesus is the Lamb of God . . .' may be substituted.

6 **The Distribution of Communion to those not present at a Celebration**
(a) This ministry to those not present at a celebration may be exercised by any ordained person, or it may be entrusted to any lay person authorized by the bishop to assist in the distribution of Holy Communion.

(b) When the consecrated bread and wine are to be conveyed directly from a celebration to those not present, they are given to the ministers after the breaking of the bread, or after the distribution, or at the end of the service.

(c) The minister who distributes communion to those who are absent from a celebration may receive communion at the same time, but need not do so.

7 **Reception of the Consecrated Bread and Wine** Communion should normally be received in both kinds separately, but where necessary may be received in either of the following ways:
(a) by intinction, in which case the minister says 'The body and blood...';
(b) in one kind, whether of bread or, where the communicant cannot receive solid food, wine.

8 **Spiritual Communion** Believers who cannot physically receive the sacraments are to be assured that they are partakers by faith of the body and blood of Christ and of the benefits he conveys to us by them.

A FORM OF PERSONAL PREPARATION

1 Jesus says: I am the bread of life. Whoever comes to me shall never be hungry and whoever believes in me shall never be thirsty. I am that living bread which has come down from heaven; if anyone eats this bread he shall live for ever. Moreover, the bread which I will give is my own flesh; I give it for the life of the world. *John 6.33, 51*

2 Arrangements have been made for you to receive Holy Communion. You will be sharing in Communion with patients in hospitals and at home and with people in churches, as surely as if you were present alongside them, for in this sacrament you are united with the whole Body of Christ.

3 In Holy Communion Jesus gives us his life. We ought therefore to prepare ourselves and also give him thanks. You may wish to think about some of these words:

I am the bread of life.

Be still and know that I am God.

Lo, I am with you always.

He was made known to them in the breaking of the bread.

4 THANKSGIVING

Thank God for all the many blessings you have received and for all that is at present being done for you; for all doctors and nurses; (for this hospital and all who work here).

5 REPENTANCE

Ask God's forgiveness for the ways in which you have failed him and others.

6 INTERCESSION

Pray for all those you love; (for the other patients in your ward, especially those who will be receiving Communion with you;) for all who look after you; for all in need; and for yourself, that your sickness may bring you closer to God and his healing power.

7 Lord Jesus Christ,
you came to the poor and powerless
and gave them hope.
Come to me in this wonderful mystery
and raise me up in love to you,
for I am helpless on my own.

8 Almighty and everlasting God,
we approach the sacrament of your only-begotten
Son, our Lord Jesus Christ.
As sick, we come to the physician of life;
as unclean, to the fountain of mercy;
as blind, to the light of eternal splendour;
as needy, to the Lord of heaven and earth;
as naked, to the King of glory.
St Thomas Aquinas

9 Be calm in the knowledge that you are under the protection of almighty God.

The Celebration of the Holy Communion in the presence of the Sick Rite A

1 The president greets the people with the following or other appropriate words.

Peace to this house and to all who live in it.

or The peace of the Lord be always with you.

2 This prayer may be said.

All **Almighty God,
to whom all hearts are open,
all desires known,
and from whom no secrets are hidden:
cleanse the thoughts of our hearts
by the inspiration of your Holy Spirit,
that we may perfectly love you,
and worthily magnify your holy name;
through Christ our Lord. Amen.**

3 The president says the COLLECT of the day, or another appropriate collect. Further collects are to be found on ASB p. 929.

4 One or more readings from scripture may be used; a Gospel reading should normally be included. The readings may be those of the season or be taken from the Appendix. Any sermon should be brief and suitable to the occasion.

5 Appropriate intercessions may be made.

6 Minister Hear the words of comfort our Saviour Christ
says to all who truly turn to him:
Come to me, all who labour and are heavy laden,
and I will give you rest. *Matthew 11.28*

God so loved the world that he gave his only Son, that whoever believes in him should not perish but have eternal life. *John 3.16*

7 Minister

Let us confess our sins, in penitence and faith,
firmly resolved to keep God's commandments
and to live in love and peace with all men.

8 **All**

Almighty God, our heavenly Father,
we have sinned against you and against our fellow men,
in thought and word and deed,
through negligence, through weakness,
through our own deliberate fault.
We are truly sorry
and repent of all our sins.
For the sake of your Son Jesus Christ, who died for us,
forgive us all that is past;
and grant that we may serve you in newness of life
to the glory of your name. Amen.

9 President

Almighty God,
who forgives all who truly repent,
have mercy upon you,
pardon and deliver you from all your sins,
confirm and strengthen you in all goodness,
and keep you in life eternal;
through Jesus Christ our Lord. **Amen.**

10 All may say

We do not presume
to come to this your table, merciful Lord,
trusting in our own righteousness,
but in your manifold and great mercies.
We are not worthy
so much as to gather up the crumbs under your table.

But you are the same Lord
whose nature is always to have mercy.
Grant us therefore, gracious Lord,
so to eat the flesh of your dear Son
Jesus Christ and to drink his blood,
that we may evermore dwell in him
and he in us. Amen.

11 *The president takes the bread and wine.*

12	President	The Lord be with you *or*	The Lord is here.
	All	**and also with you.**	**His Spirit is with us.**

President Lift up your hearts.
All **We lift them to the Lord.**

President Let us give thanks to the Lord our God.
All **It is right to give him thanks and praise.**

President It is indeed right,
it is our duty and our joy,
to give you thanks, holy Father,
through Jesus Christ our Lord.

Through him you have created us in your image;
through him you have freed us from sin and death;
through him you have made us your own people
by the gift of the Holy Spirit.

Hear us, Father,
through Christ your Son our Lord,
and grant that by the power of your Holy Spirit
these gifts of bread and wine
may be to us his body and his blood;

Who in the same night that he was betrayed,
took bread and gave you thanks;
he broke it and gave it to his disciples, saying,
Take, eat; this is my body which is given for you;
do this in remembrance of me.

In the same way, after supper
he took the cup and gave you thanks;
he gave it to them, saying,
Drink this, all of you;
this is my blood of the new covenant,
which is shed for you and for many for the
forgiveness of sins.
Do this, as often as you drink it,
in remembrance of me.

Therefore, Father,
proclaiming his saving death and resurrection
and looking for his coming in glory,
we celebrate with this bread and this cup
his one perfect sacrifice.

Accept through him, our great high priest,
this our sacrifice of thanks and praise;
and grant that we who eat this bread and drink
this cup
may be renewed by your Spirit and grow into
his likeness;

Through Jesus Christ our Lord,
by whom, and with whom, and in whom,
all honour and glory be yours, Father,
now and for ever. **Amen.**

13 THE LORD'S PRAYER is said either as follows or in its traditional form.

President As our Saviour taught us, so we pray.
All **Our Father in heaven,**
hallowed be your name,
your kingdom come,
your will be done,
on earth as in heaven.
Give us today our daily bread.
Forgive us our sins
as we forgive those who sin against us.

Lead us not into temptation
but deliver us from evil.

For the kingdom, the power, and the glory
are yours
now and for ever. Amen.

14 The president breaks the consecrated bread, saying

We break this bread
to share in the body of Christ.

All **Though we are many, we are one body,**
because we all share in one bread.

15 Before the distribution the president says

Draw near with faith. Receive the body of our Lord Jesus Christ which he gave for you, and his blood which he shed for you.

Eat and drink in remembrance that he died for you, and feed on him in your *hearts* by faith with thanksgiving.

The president may also say

Jesus is the Lamb of God
who takes away the sins of the world.
Happy are those who are called to his supper.

All **Lord, I am not worthy to receive you,**
but only say the word, and I shall be healed.

16 The president and people receive the communion. At the distribution the minister says any authorized words.

17 After communion this or another appropriate prayer is said.

All **Almighty God,**
we thank you for feeding us
with the body and blood of your Son
Jesus Christ.

Through him we offer you our souls and bodies
to be a living sacrifice.
Strengthen us
in the power of your Spirit
to live and work
to your praise and glory. Amen.

18 President The peace of God, which passes all understanding, keep your hearts and minds in the knowledge and love of God, and of his Son Jesus Christ our Lord; and the blessing of God almighty, the Father, the Son, and the Holy Spirit, be among you, and remain with you always. **Amen.**

The Celebration of the Holy Communion in the presence of the Sick Rite B

1 The priest greets the people with the following or other appropriate words.

Peace to this house and to all who live in it.

or The peace of the Lord be always with you.

2 This prayer may be said.

All **Almighty God,**
unto whom all hearts be open,
all desires known,
and from whom no secrets are hid:
cleanse the thoughts of our hearts
by the inspiration of thy Holy Spirit,
that we may perfectly love thee,
and worthily magnify thy holy name;
through Christ our Lord. Amen.

3 The priest says the COLLECT of the day, or another appropriate collect. Further collects are to be found on ASB p. 929.

4 One or more readings from scripture may be used; a Gospel reading should normally be included. The readings may be those of the season or be taken from the Appendix. Any sermon should be brief and suitable to the occasion.

5 Appropriate intercessions may be made.

6 Priest Hear what comfortable words our Saviour Christ says to all who truly turn to him:
Come unto me, all that travail, and are heavy laden, and I will refresh you. *Matthew 11.28*

So God loved the world, that he gave his only-begotten Son, to the end that all that believe in him should not perish, but have everlasting life. *John 3.16*

7 Priest

Seeing we have a great high priest who has passed into the heavens, Jesus the Son of God, let us draw near with a true heart, in full assurance of faith, and make our confession to our heavenly Father.

8 **All**

Almighty God, our heavenly Father,
we have sinned against thee,
through our own fault,
in thought, and word, and deed,
and in what we have left undone.
We are heartily sorry
and repent of all our sins.
For thy Son our Lord Jesus Christ's sake,
forgive us all that is past;
and grant that we may serve thee in newness of life,
to the glory of thy name. Amen.

9 Priest

Almighty God,
who forgives all who truly repent,
have mercy upon *you*,
pardon and deliver *you* from all *your* sins,
confirm and strengthen *you* in all goodness,
and keep *you* in life eternal;
through Jesus Christ our Lord. **Amen.**

10 All may say

We do not presume
to come to this thy table, O merciful Lord,
trusting in our own righteousness,
but in thy manifold and great mercies.
We are not worthy
so much as to gather up the crumbs under thy table.

But thou art the same Lord
whose nature is always to have mercy.
Grant us therefore, gracious Lord,
so to eat the flesh of thy dear Son
Jesus Christ
and to drink his blood,
that we may evermore dwell in him
and he in us. Amen.

11 The priest takes the bread and wine.

12 Priest The Lord be with you
All **and with thy spirit.**

Priest Lift up your hearts.
All **We lift them up unto the Lord.**

Priest Let us give thanks unto the Lord our God.
All **It is meet and right so to do.**

Priest It is very meet, right, and our bounden duty,
that we should give thanks unto thee, holy Father,
through Jesus Christ our Lord.

Because through him thou hast created us
in thine image;
through him thou didst redeem us from sin
and death;
through him thou hast made us thine own people
by the gift of thy Holy Spirit.

Hear us, O Father,
through Christ thy Son our Lord;
and grant that by the power of thy Holy Spirit
these gifts of bread and wine
may be unto us his body and blood.

Who, in the same night that he was betrayed,
took bread;
Here the priest is to take the bread into his hands.

and when he had given thanks to thee,
he broke it,
and gave it to his disciples, saying, Take, eat;
this is my body which is given for you:
do this in remembrance of me.

Likewise after supper he took the cup;
Here he is to take the cup into his hands.
and when he had given thanks to thee,
he gave it to them, saying, Drink ye all of this;
for this is my blood of the new covenant,
which is shed for you and for many
for the remission of sins:
do this, as oft as ye shall drink it,
in remembrance of me.

Wherefore, Father, having in remembrance
his saving death and resurrection,
and looking for the coming of his kingdom,
we make with this bread and this cup
the memorial of Christ thy Son our Lord.

Accept this our sacrifice of praise and thanksgiving
and grant that we may so eat and drink
these holy gifts
that we may be filled with thy grace
and heavenly blessing;

Through Jesus Christ our Lord,
by whom, and with whom, and in whom,
in the unity of the Holy Spirit,
all honour and glory be unto thee,
O Father almighty,
world without end. **Amen.**

13 THE LORD'S PRAYER is said.

Priest As our Saviour has taught us, so we pray.
**All Our Father, who art in heaven,
hallowed be thy name;
thy kingdom come;
thy will be done;
on earth as it is in heaven.**

Give us this day our daily bread.
And forgive us our trespasses,
as we forgive those who trespass
against us.
And lead us not into temptation;
but deliver us from evil.

For thine is the kingdom, the power,
and the glory,
for ever and ever. Amen.

14 The priest breaks the consecrated bread, saying

We break this bread
to share in the body of Christ

All **Though we are many, we are one body,**
because we all share in one bread.

15 Before the distribution the priest says

Draw near and receive the body of our Lord Jesus Christ, which was given for you, and his blood, which was shed for you. Take this in remembrance that Christ died for you, and feed on him in your *hearts* by faith with thanksgiving.

16 The president and people receive the communion. At the distribution the minister says any authorized words.

17 After communion this or another appropriate prayer is said.

All **Almighty God,**
we thank thee for feeding us
with the body and blood of thy Son
Jesus Christ our Lord.
Through him we offer thee our souls
and bodies to be a living sacrifice.
Strengthen us
in the power of thy Spirit
to live and work
to thy praise and glory. Amen.

18 Priest — The peace of God, which passes all understanding, keep your hearts and minds in the knowledge and love of God, and of his Son Jesus Christ our Lord; and the blessing of God almighty, the Father, the Son, and the Holy Spirit, be among you and remain with you always. **Amen.**

The Distribution of Communion to those not present at a Celebration Rite A

1 The minister greets the people with the following or other appropriate words.

Peace to this house and to all who live in it.

or The peace of the Lord be always with you.

2 This prayer may be said.

All **Almighty God,**
to whom all hearts are open,
all desires known,
and from whom no secrets are hidden:
cleanse the thoughts of our hearts
by the inspiration of your Holy Spirit,
that we may perfectly love you,
and worthily magnify your holy name;
through Christ our Lord. Amen.

3 The minister says the COLLECT of the day, or another appropriate collect. Further collects are to be found on ASB p. 929.

4 One or more readings from scripture may be used; a Gospel reading should normally be included. The readings may be those of the season or be taken from the Appendix. Any sermon should be brief and suitable to the occasion.

5 Appropriate intercessions may be made.

6 Minister Let us confess our sins, in penitence and faith,
firmly resolved to keep God's commandments
and to live in love and peace with all men.

7 **All**

Almighty God, our heavenly Father,
we have sinned against you and against our fellow men,
in thought and word and deed,
through negligence, through weakness,
through our own deliberate fault.
We are truly sorry
and repent of all our sins.
For the sake of your Son Jesus Christ, who died for us.
forgive us all that is past;
and grant that we may serve you in newness of life
to the glory of your name. Amen.

8 Minister

Almighty God,
who forgives all who truly repent,
have mercy upon *you,*
pardon and deliver *you* from all *your* sins,
confirm and strengthen *you* in all goodness,
and keep *you* in life eternal;
through Jesus Christ our Lord. **Amen.**

9 All may say

We do not presume
to come to this your table, merciful Lord,
trusting in our own righteousness,
but in your manifold and great mercies.
We are not worthy
so much as to gather up the crumbs under your table.
But you are the same Lord
whose nature is always to have mercy.
Grant us therefore, gracious Lord,
so to eat the flesh of your dear Son Jesus Christ and to drink his blood,
that we may evermore dwell in him
and he in us. Amen.

10 The minister explains this ministry of communion using the following or other suitable words.

The Church of God, of which we are members, has taken bread and wine and given thanks over them according to our Lord's command. I bring these holy gifts that you may share in the communion of his body and blood. We who are many are one body, because we all share in one bread.

11 THE LORD'S PRAYER is said either as follows or in its traditional form.

Minister As our Saviour taught us, so we pray.

All **Our Father in heaven,**
hallowed be your name,
your kingdom come,
your will be done,
on earth as in heaven.
Give us today our daily bread.
Forgive us our sins
as we forgive those who sin against us.
Lead us not into temptation
but deliver us from evil.

For the kingdom, the power, and the glory
are yours
now and for ever. Amen.

12 Before the distribution the minister says

Draw near with faith. Receive the body of our Lord Jesus Christ which he gave for you, and his blood which he shed for you.

Eat and drink in remembrance that he died for you, and feed on him in your *hearts* by faith with thanksgiving.

The minister may also say

Jesus is the Lamb of God
who takes away the sins of the world.
Happy are those who are called to his supper.

All **Lord, I am not worthy to receive you,**
but only say the word, and I shall be healed.

13 At the distribution the minister says any authorized words.

14 After communion this or another appropriate prayer is said.

All **Almighty God,**
we thank you for feeding us
with the body and blood of your Son
Jesus Christ.
Through him we offer you our souls and bodies
to be a living sacrifice.
Strengthen us
in the power of your Spirit
to live and work
to your praise and glory. Amen.

15 The minister may say the Grace or an appropriate blessing.

The grace of our Lord Jesus Christ, and the love of God, and the fellowship of the Holy Spirit be with us all evermore. **Amen.**

The Distribution of Communion to those not present at a Celebration Rite B

1 The minister greets the people with the following or other appropriate words.

Peace to this house and to all who live in it.

or The peace of the Lord be always with you.

2 This prayer may be said.

All **Almighty God,**
unto whom all hearts be open,
all desires known,
and from whom no secrets are hid:
cleanse the thoughts of our hearts
by the inspiration of thy Holy Spirit,
that we may perfectly love thee,
and worthily magnify thy holy name;
through Christ our Lord. Amen.

3 The minister says the COLLECT of the day, or another appropriate collect. Further collects are to be found on ASB p. 929.

4 One or more readings from scripture may be used; a Gospel reading should normally be included. The readings may be those of the season or be taken from the Appendix. Any sermon should be brief and suitable to the occasion.

5 Appropriate intercessions may be made.

6 Minister Seeing we have a great high priest who has passed into the heavens, Jesus the Son of God, let us draw near with a true heart, in full assurance of faith, and make our confession to our heavenly Father.

7 **All** **Almighty God, our heavenly Father,**
we have sinned against thee,
through our own fault,
in thought, and word, and deed,
and in what we have left undone.
We are heartily sorry
and repent of all our sins.
For thy Son our Lord Jesus Christ's sake,
forgive us all that is past;
and grant that we may serve thee in newness of life,
to the glory of thy name. Amen.

8 Minister Almighty God,
who forgives all who truly repent,
have mercy upon *you,*
pardon and deliver *you* from all *your* sins,
confirm and strengthen *you* in all goodness,
and keep *you* in life eternal;
through Jesus Christ our Lord. **Amen.**

9 All may say

We do not presume
to come to this thy table, O merciful Lord,
trusting in our own righteousness,
but in thy manifold and great mercies.
We are not worthy
so much as to gather up the crumbs under thy table.
But thou art the same Lord
whose nature is always to have mercy.
Grant us therefore, gracious Lord,
so to eat the flesh of thy dear Son Jesus Christ
and to drink his blood,
that we may evermore dwell in him
and he in us. Amen.

10 The minister explains this ministry of communion using the following or other suitable words.

The Church of God, of which we are members, has taken bread and wine and given thanks over them according to our Lord's command. I bring these holy gifts that you may share in the communion of his body and blood. We who are many are one body, because we all share in one bread.

11 THE LORD'S PRAYER is said.

Minister As our Saviour has taught us, so we pray.
All **Our Father, who art in heaven,**
hallowed be thy name;
thy kingdom come;
thy will be done;
on earth as it is in heaven.
Give us this day our daily bread.
And forgive us our trespasses,
as we forgive those who trespass
against us.
And lead us not into temptation;
but deliver us from evil.

For thine is the kingdom, the power,
and the glory,
for ever and ever. Amen.

12 Before the distribution the minister says

Draw near and receive the body of our Lord Jesus Christ, which was given for you, and his blood, which was shed for you. Take this in remembrance that Christ died for you, and feed on him in your hearts by faith with thanksgiving.

13 At the distribution the minister says any authorized words.

14 After communion this or another appropriate prayer is said.

All **Almighty God,**
we thank thee for feeding us
with the body and blood of thy Son
Jesus Christ our Lord.
Through him we offer thee our souls
and bodies to be a living sacrifice.
Strengthen us
in the power of thy Spirit
to live and work
to thy praise and glory. Amen.

15 The minister may say the Grace or an appropriate blessing.

The grace of our Lord Jesus Christ, and the love of God, and the fellowship of the Holy Spirit be with us all evermore. **Amen.**

The Laying on of Hands with Prayer, and Anointing

NOTES

1 **Modification** The president at his discretion may vary the order provided.

2 **Preparation** Careful devotional preparation before the use of these ministries is recommended.

3 **The Ministry in Hospital** Where these services take place in a hospital, the co-operation of the staff should be sought.

4 **Seasonal Material** Provision of proper collects, readings, and psalms is made in the order following. The seasonal or Sunday provision may be used in place of that set out here. At Christmas, Easter, and Pentecost some at least of the seasonal provision for the Festival should be used.

5 **Explanation** An explanation of the particular ministry which is being used should be given, and this may come at the beginning of the service, or as part of the sermon, or immediately after the sermon. The form provided at section 7 may be used, or the minister may use his own words.

6 **The Needs of the Sick** If desired, at an appropriate place in the service, the physical condition and needs of the sick may be declared to the congregation in order to guide their prayers.

7 **The President** The president of the eucharist also presides over the ministry of laying on of hands and anointing of the sick. He may invite others to share with him in the prayers and the laying on of hands, and may delegate the ministry of anointing to other lawful ministers. When the context of the service is Morning or Evening Prayer or any other service than the eucharist, a deacon or authorized lay minister may preside over the ministry of the laying on of hands.

8 **The Distribution of Communion to those not present at a Celebration** The order here provided may be adapted to conform with the distribution of communion to those not present at a celebration.

9 **Anointing of the Sick** Anointing is a sacramental ministry, authorized by Canon B37, which provides that if a sick person 'so desires, the priest may lay hands upon him and may anoint him with oil on the forehead with the sign of the Cross'. It should be used more sparingly than the laying on of hands, and is especially appropriate for use when a sick person is at a time of crisis. As provided by Canon B37, the laying on of hands may suitably be used in association with anointing.

10 **The Oil of Anointing** Canon B37 provides that the priest should use 'pure olive oil consecrated by the bishop of the diocese or otherwise by the priest himself...'

11 **The Anointing** Canon B37 provides that the anointing should be made on the forehead with the sign of the cross, but other parts of the body may be anointed in addition to the forehead.

12 **Silence** Silence may be kept at appropriate points within the liturgical order at the discretion of the president.

The Laying on of Hands with Prayer, and Anointing, at the Holy Communion

THE INTRODUCTION

1 THIS SENTENCE may be used.

Truly the Lord has borne our sufferings and carried our sorrows. *Isaiah 53.4*

2 The president greets the people using these or other appropriate words.

The Lord be with you
All **and also with you.**

3 Then may be said

Lord Jesus, you healed the sick:
Lord, have mercy.
Lord, have mercy.

Lord Jesus, you forgave sinners:
Christ, have mercy.
Christ, have mercy.

Lord Jesus, you gave yourself to heal us
and bring us strength:
Lord, have mercy.
Lord, have mercy.

4 The president says one of the following COLLECTS.

Heavenly Father,
you anointed your Son Jesus Christ
with the Holy Spirit and with power
to bring to man the blessings of your kingdom.
Anoint your Church with the same Holy Spirit,
that we who share in his suffering and his victory
may bear witness to the gospel of salvation;
through Jesus Christ our Lord. **Amen.**

or Almighty God, the fountain of all wisdom,
you know our needs before we ask
and our ignorance in asking;
have compassion on our weakness,
and give us those things
which for our unworthiness we dare not
and for our blindness we cannot ask,
for the sake of your Son, Jesus Christ our Lord.
Amen.

THE MINISTRY OF THE WORD

5 Either two or three readings from scripture follow, the last of which is always the Gospel.

A CANTICLE, A HYMN or A PSALM may be used between the readings.

6 A SERMON may be preached.

THE LAYING ON OF HANDS AND ANOINTING

7 One of the ministers may explain this ministry, using one or both of these paragraphs or his own words.

Our Lord Jesus Christ went about preaching the gospel and healing. He commanded his disciples to lay hands on the sick that they might be healed. Following his example, and in obedience to his command, we shall lay hands on *N*, praying that the Lord will grant healing and peace according to his loving and gracious will.

Saint James writes, 'Is any among you sick? Let him call for the elders of the church, and let them pray over him, anointing him with oil in the name of the Lord; and the prayer of faith will save the sick man, and the Lord will raise him up; and if he has committed sins he will be forgiven.' In fulfilment of this we shall anoint *N* with oil, praying that the Lord will grant healing and restoration and forgiveness according to his loving and gracious will.

THE PRAYERS

8 Intercessions are made, particularly for the sick. This form may be used.

Minister Come, Lord, with your love and mercy in this ministry, and comfort the distressed. Free *him* from all harm.
All **Lord, hear our prayer.**

Minister Relieve *his* suffering: sustain *him* with your power.
All **Lord, hear our prayer.**

Minister Give new strength to *his* body, mind, and spirit.
All **Lord, hear our prayer.**

Minister In your name we lay our hands on (anoint) *N*. Give *him* the assurance of your presence, and your peace.
All **Lord, have mercy. Amen.**

9 Minister Hear the words of comfort our Saviour Christ says to all who truly turn to him:
Come to me, all who labour and are heavy laden, and I will give you rest. *Matthew 11.28*

God so loved the world that he gave his only Son, that whoever believes in him should not perish but have eternal life. *John 3.16*

10 Minister Let us confess our sins, in penitence and faith, firmly resolved to keep God's commandments and to live in love and peace with all men.

11 **All** **Almighty God, our heavenly Father,**
we have sinned against you and against our fellow men,
in thought and word and deed,
through negligence, through weakness,
through our own deliberate fault.
We are truly sorry
and repent of all our sins.
For the sake of your Son Jesus Christ, who died for us,
forgive us all that is past;
and grant that we may serve you in newness of life
to the glory of your name. Amen.

12 Minister Almighty God,
who forgives all who truly repent,
have mercy upon *you*,
pardon and deliver *you* from all *your* sins,
confirm and strengthen *you* in all goodness,
and keep *you* in life eternal;
through Jesus Christ our Lord. **Amen.**

THE LAYING ON OF HANDS

13 At the laying on of hands these or other suitable words are used. If anointing is to follow, the laying on of hands may be done in silence.

In the name of our Lord Jesus Christ who laid his hands on the sick that they might be healed *I* lay *my* hands upon you, *N.* May almighty God, Father, Son, and Holy Spirit, make you whole in body, mind, and spirit, give you light and peace, and keep you in life eternal. **Amen.**

THE ANOINTING

14 If anointing is also to take place the priest makes the sign of the cross on the sick person, using these or other similar words.

N, I anoint you with oil in the name of our Lord Jesus Christ. May our heavenly Father make you whole in body and mind, and grant you the inward anointing of his Holy Spirit, the Spirit of strength and joy and peace. **Amen.**

15 This or some other appropriate prayer may be said.

Priest The almighty Lord, who is a strong tower to all who put their trust in him, be now and evermore your defence, and make you believe and trust that the only name under heaven given for health and salvation is the name of our Lord Jesus Christ. **Amen.**

THE COMMUNION

16 The president resumes the Holy Communion at THE PEACE (Holy Communion Rite A, sections 30, 31; Rite B, sections 24, 25).

17 These special forms are used.

PROPER PREFACE

And now we give you thanks because in his victory over the grave a new age has dawned, the long reign of sin is ended, a broken world is being renewed, and man is once again made whole.

or And now we give you thanks because through him you have given us eternal life, and delivered us from the bondage of sin and the fear of death into the glorious liberty of the children of God.

POSTCOMMUNION SENTENCE

O praise the Lord.
He heals the broken in spirit
and binds up their wounds. *Psalm 147.1, 3*

ALTERNATIVE BLESSING

The Lord bless you and watch over you,
The Lord make his face to shine upon you
and be gracious to you,
the Lord look kindly on you and give you peace;
and the blessing of God Almighty,
the Father, the Son, and the Holy Spirit,
be among you and remain with you always. **Amen.**

The Laying on of Hands with Prayer, and Anointing, at Morning or Evening Prayer

When the Service is used at Morning or Evening Prayer, proper psalms and readings may be used, and the sentence (section 1) and the collect (section 4) may be used instead of those of the day. The Service follows this order.

Order	Service	Section
Introduction	MP, EP	1, 24*
Sentence	LH	1
Responses	MP, EP	8, 31
Invitatory	MP, EP	9, 32
Psalm	MP, EP	10, 33
Reading	MP, EP	11, 34
Canticle	MP, EP	12, 35
Reading	MP, EP	13, 36
Sermon	LH	6
Explanation	LH	7
Intercessions	LH	8, 9
Penitence	LH	10-12
Laying on of hands and anointing	LH	13-15
Canticle	MP, EP	**
Creed	MP, EP	16, 39
Prayers	MP, EP	17-23, 40-46

* This special form is used.

We have come together as the family of God
in our Father's presence
to offer him praise and thanksgiving,
to hear and receive his holy word,
to bring before him the needs of the world,
to ask his forgiveness of our sins
and his healing of the sick,
and to seek his grace,
that through his Son Jesus Christ
we may give ourselves to his service.

** Great and Wonderful, Nunc Dimittis, or Saviour of the World.

When the Service is not combined with any other, sections 1–16 are used. There follows:

	Te Deum
or	General Thanksgiving (ASB p. 104)
or	Psalm 103 Prayer (ASB p. 173) Blessing (section 17)

A Commendation at the Time of Death

Note These prayers are set out in the form of a service for a dying person and for family and friends gathered at a death-bed. They may be led by a priest or by any other Christian person. The commendation may be accompanied by the making of the sign of the cross by those present on the forehead of the dying person, recalling his baptism into Christ.

1 In the name of the Father and of the Son
and of the Holy Spirit. **Amen.**

2 Lord have mercy upon us.

Christ, have mercy upon us.

Lord, have mercy upon us.

3 The Lord's Prayer is said either as follows or in its traditional form.

**Our Father in heaven,
hallowed be your name,
your kingdom come,
your will be done,
on earth as in heaven.
Give us today our daily bread.
Forgive us our sins
as we forgive those who sin against us.
Lead us not into temptation
but deliver us from evil.**

**For the kingdom, the power, and the glory
are yours
now and for ever. Amen.**

4 One of the following or other appropriate passages of scripture may be read.

Jesus said, 'Let not your hearts be troubled; believe in God, believe also in me. In my Father's house are many rooms; if it were not so, would I have told you that I go to prepare a place for you? And when I go and prepare a place for you, I will come again and take you to myself, that where I am you may be also. Peace I leave with you; my peace I give you. I do not give to you as the world gives. Do not let your hearts be troubled and do not be afraid'.
John 14.1-3, 27

None of us lives to himself, and none of us dies to himself. If we live, we live to the Lord, and if we die, we die to the Lord; so then, whether we live or whether we die, we are the Lord's. For to this end Christ died and lived again, that he might be Lord both of the dead and of the living. *Romans 14.7-9*

5 These responses, or a psalm, may be said.

Into your hands, O Lord, I commit my spirit.
Into your hands, O Lord, I commit my spirit.

You will redeem me, O Lord God of truth.
I commit my spirit.

Glory to the Father, and to the Son,
and to the Holy Spirit.
Into your hands, O Lord, I commit my spirit.

Keep me as the apple of your eye.
Hide me under the shadow of your wings.

6 Either of the following prayers may be said.

Into your hands, Lord,
our faithful creator and most loving redeemer,
we commend your child *N*,
for *he* is yours in death as in life.
In your great mercy
fulfil in *him* the purpose of your love;
gather *him* to yourself in gentleness and peace,
that, rejoicing in the light
and refreshment of your presence,
he may enjoy that rest which you have prepared
for your faithful servants;
through Jesus Christ our Lord. **Amen.**

or

Lord Jesus Christ,
by the love of your eternal Father,
and by your own last words
commending your spirit to him,
welcome *N*, your child,
that, being dead to the world,
he may live to you alone,
and for ever enjoy the perfect vision of your glory.
Amen.

7 Either of the following commendations may be said.

Go forth upon your journey from this world,
O Christian soul,
in the name of God the Father almighty
who created you;
in the name of Jesus Christ
who suffered death for you;
in the name of the Holy Spirit, who strengthens you;
in communion with the blessed saints,
and aided by angels and archangels,
and all the armies of the heavenly host.
May your portion this day be in peace,
and your dwelling the heavenly Jerusalem. **Amen.**

or

N, our companion in faith,
the Lord who gave you to us
is taking you to himself.
He who died for you and rose again from death,
is calling you to enjoy the peace of the heavenly city
in which there is neither sorrow nor pain,
and where weakness is transformed into strength.
He is calling you to see him face to face
that you may be made like him for ever.
He comes to welcome you
with angels and archangels
and all his faithful people
that you may know in its fullness the fellowship
of the Holy Spirit.
Enter into the joy of your Lord
and give glory to him,
Father, Son, and Holy Spirit. **Amen.**

8 This prayer may be said.

Lord Jesus Christ, Son of the living God,
remember your last hour
when on the cross you gave up your spirit
to your Father.
Set your passion, cross, and death
between your judgement and us.
As we entrust *N* to you
we pray you to free us all from the pains of death
and from all wounds of sin,
that death may be the gate to life
and to unending fellowship with you,
for you are the Resurrection and the Life;
to you be glory for ever. **Amen.**

9 After the death one or more of the following sentences and prayers may be said. Other suitable prayers are in sections 26-28 on p. 49.

10 The Lord gave and the Lord has taken away: blessed be the name of the Lord. *Job 1.21*

Jesus said 'I am the resurrection and the life; he who believes in me, though he die, yet shall he live.' *John 11.25*

Neither death, nor life, nor angels, nor principalities, nor powers, nor things present, nor things to come, nor height, nor depth, nor anything else in all creation, will be able to separate us from the love of God in Christ Jesus our Lord. *Romans 8.38, 39*

In your presence is the fullness of joy: at your right hand there are pleasures for evermore. *Psalm 16.11*

Blessed are those who die in the Lord. Even so, says the Spirit, for they rest from their labours. *Revelation 14.13*

11 Almighty and merciful Father, we give you thanks for the life of your servant *N*; and we pray that, preserving the good of *his* example among us, you will guard your truth from generation to generation; through Jesus Christ our Lord. **Amen.**

12 O Lord Jesus Christ, God of all consolation, whose heart was moved to tears at the grave of Lazarus; look with compassion on your children in their loss. Strengthen in them the gift of faith, and give to their troubled hearts, and to the hearts of all, the light of hope, that they may live as one day to be united again, where tears shall be wiped away, in the kingdom of your love; for you died and were raised to life with the Father and the Holy Spirit, God, now and for ever. **Amen.**

13 Heavenly Father, grant us grace to use our time
aright and to live each day as those who too must
die, that in life and death we may yield ourselves into
your hands as to a faithful creator, through Jesus
Christ our Lord. **Amen.**

14 This blessing may be said.

God grant you to share in the inheritance of his
saints in glory; and the blessing of God almighty, the
Father, the Son, and the Holy Spirit, rest upon you,
and remain with you always. **Amen.**

Prayers for use with the Sick

1 Heavenly Father, giver of life and health: comfort and restore those who are sick, that they may be strengthened in their weakness, and trust in your unfailing love; through Jesus Christ our Lord. **Amen.**

2 Father, we pray for those who are mentally ill, for all who are of a disturbed and troubled mind. Be to them light in their darkness, their refuge and strength in time of fear: that they may put themselves into your hands and be filled with your peace. Give special skills and tender hearts to all who care for them, and show them how best to assist in your work of healing; through Jesus Christ our Lord. **Amen.**

3 Lord Jesus Christ, in the days of your flesh the sick were brought to you for healing: hear us as we now bring to you in our prayers those who are ill, in body or mind. May your presence be with them to relieve suffering and distress, and to restore them to fullness of life; for your great love's sake. **Amen.**

4 THE 'JESUS PRAYER'

Lord Jesus Christ,
Son of God,
have mercy on me,
a sinner.

5 ACT OF COMMITMENT

My God, I am not my own but yours.

Take me for your own
and help me in all things to do your holy will.

My God, I give myself to you,
in joy and in sorrow,

in sickness and in health,
in success and in failure,
in life and in death,
in time and for eternity. **Amen.**

6 UNION WITH CHRIST (ANIMA CHRISTI)

Soul of Christ, sanctify me.
Body of Christ, save me.
Blood of Christ, refresh me.
Water from the side of Christ, wash me.
Passion of Christ, strengthen me.
O good Jesus, hear me.
Within your wounds hide me.
Let me never be separated from you.
From the power of darkness defend me.
In the hour of my death, call me
  and bid me come to you,
that with your saints I may praise you
  for ever and ever. **Amen.**

7 ACT OF FAITH

I believe and trust in God the Father,
  who made the world.
I believe and trust in his Son Jesus Christ,
  who redeemed mankind.
I believe and trust in his Holy Spirit,
  who gives life to the people of God.

8 ST PATRICK'S BREASTPLATE

Christ be with me, Christ within me,
Christ behind me, Christ before me,
Christ beside me, Christ to win me,
Christ to comfort and restore me,
Christ beneath me, Christ above me,
Christ in quiet, Christ in danger,
Christ in hearts of all that love me,
Christ in mouth of friend and stranger.

9 PRAYER ATTRIBUTED TO ST RICHARD OF CHICHESTER

Lord Jesus Christ, we thank you
for all the benefits you have won for us,
for all the pains and insults you have borne for us.
Most merciful redeemer,
friend and brother,
may we know you more clearly,
love you more dearly,
and follow you more nearly,
day by day. **Amen.**

10 GOD BE IN MY HEAD

God be in my head, and in my understanding;
God be in my eyes, and in my looking;
God be in my mouth, and in my speaking;
God be in my heart, and in my thinking;
God be at my end, and at my departing.
From the Sarum Primer

PRAYERS BEFORE AN OPERATION

11 Lord Jesus,
by the loneliness of your suffering on the cross
be near to me in my need.
Banish my fears,
increase my faith;
hold me in your love
and fill me with your peace;
for your name's sake. **Amen.**

12 God is our refuge and strength:
a very present help in trouble.
Though my flesh and my heart fail me:
you, O God, are my portion for ever.
Forsake me not, O Lord,
go not far from me, my God:
hasten to help me, O Lord my salvation.

Why are you so full of heaviness, my soul:
and why so unquiet within me?
O put your trust in God:
for I will praise him yet,
who is my deliverer and my God.

13 Cast care aside, lean on your guide;
his boundless mercy will provide;
trust, and your trusting soul shall prove
Christ is its life, and Christ its love.
After J S B Monsell

EVENING PRAYERS

14 Watch, dear Lord, with those who wake, or watch, or weep tonight, and let your angels protect those who sleep. Tend the sick. Refresh the weary. Sustain the dying. Calm the suffering. Pity the distressed. We ask this for the sake of your love. **Amen.** *St Augustine*

15 O Lord, support us all the day long of this troublous life, until the shades lengthen, and the evening comes, and the busy world is hushed, the fever of life is over, and our work is done. Then, Lord, in your mercy grant us safe lodging, a holy rest, and peace at the last; through Jesus Christ our Lord. **Amen.**
After John Henry Newman

16 Be with us, merciful God, and protect us through the silent hours of this night, that we who are wearied by the changes and chances of this fleeting world, may rest upon your eternal changelessness; through Jesus Christ our Lord. **Amen.**

17 Lighten our darkness,
Lord, we pray;
and in your mercy defend us
from all perils and dangers of this night;
for the love of your only Son,
our Saviour Jesus Christ. **Amen.**

THE MINISTRY OF HEALING

18 Almighty God, whose son Jesus Christ went about doing good and healing all kinds of illness: continue his gracious work among us in hospitals and homes and wherever his people gather. Give wisdom, sympathy and patience to those who minister to the sick, and prosper all that is being done to prevent suffering and to forward the purposes of your love; through the same Jesus Christ our Lord. **Amen.**

19 O Lord Christ, bless all whom you have called to share in your own ministry of healing. Give them skill, understanding and compassion; and in their work, help them to lean on your grace and to seek your glory. **Amen.**

PRAYERS FOR A SICK CHILD

20 Lord Jesus Christ,
you took children in your arms and blessed them.
Draw near to this child
and hold *him* in your love.
Restore *him* to health
and fill *him* with your peace;
for your name's sake. **Amen.**

21 Almighty God,
whose blessed Son Jesus Christ
   called children to himself,
lay your hand of healing upon this your child,
that according to your loving purpose
he may be restored to strength
   of body, mind, and spirit,
and live to praise your holy name;
through Jesus Christ our Lord. **Amen.**

A PRAYER FOR THE FAMILY

22 Heavenly Father,
whose love enfolds us all,
have mercy on those who must watch
the suffering of those whom they love.
Comfort them in anxiety,
sustain them in weakness,
strengthen them in faith,
and grant them your peace;
through Jesus Christ our Lord. **Amen.**

THANKSGIVING FOR THE BEGINNING OF RECOVERY

23 O Lord, your compassions never fail and your mercies are new every morning: We give you thanks for giving our *brother N* both relief from pain and hope of health renewed. Continue in *him*, we pray, the good work you have begun: that *he*, daily increasing in bodily strength, and rejoicing in your goodness, may so order *his* life and conduct that *he* may always think and do those things that please you; through Jesus Christ our Lord. **Amen.**

24 SAVIOUR OF THE WORLD

Saviour of the world, you have redeemed us by your passion and cross. Save us, and help us, we humbly pray.

PRAYERS FOR USE IMMEDIATELY AFTER A DEATH

25 Neither death, nor life, nor angels, nor principalities, nor powers, nor things present, nor things to come, nor height, nor depth, nor anything else in all creation, will be able to separate us from the love of God in Christ Jesus our Lord. *Romans 8.38, 39*

26 Lord Jesus, as you looked with love and forgiveness at the thief who died beside you on his cross, remember in your kingdom our *brother N*, and welcome *him* to be with you for ever in paradise. **Amen.**

27 Blessed be the God and Father of our Lord
Jesus Christ
who has blessed us all with the gift of this earthly life
and has given to our *brother N his* span of years and
gifts of character.
God our Father, we thank you now for all *his* life,
for every memory of love and joy,
for every good deed done by *him*
and every sorrow shared with us.
We thank you for *his* life and for *his* death,
we thank you for the rest in Christ *he* now enjoys,
we thank you for giving *him* to us and for taking *him*
back to yourself,
we thank you for the glory we shall share together.
Hear our prayers through Jesus Christ our Lord.
Amen.

28 God our Father, we thank you for all *N's* life;
we thank you that *he* is yours in both life and death.
Grant that in Christ we may share with *him* in your
eternal glory;
through the same Jesus Christ our Lord. **Amen.**

Appendix: Psalms and Readings

PSALM 23

The Lord is my shepherd:
  therefore can I lack nothing.

He will make me lie down in green pastures:
  and lead me beside still waters.

He will refresh my soul:
  and guide me in right pathways for his name's sake.

Though I walk through the valley of the shadow of death,
I will fear no evil:
  for you are with me,
  your rod and your staff comfort me.

You spread a table before me
in the face of those who trouble me:
  you have anointed my head with oil,
  and my cup will be full.

Surely your goodness and loving-kindness
will follow me all the days of my life:
  and I shall dwell in the house of the Lord for ever.

PSALM 46

God is our refuge and strength:
  a very present help in trouble.

Therefore we will not fear though the earth be moved:
  and though the mountains are shaken in the
  midst of the sea;

though the waters rage and foam:
  and though the mountains quake at the rising of the sea.

There is a river whose streams make glad the city of God:
  the holy dwelling-place of the Most High.

God is in the midst of her, therefore she shall not be moved:
  God will help her, and at break of day.

The nations make uproar, and the kingdoms are shaken:
but God has lifted his voice, and the earth shall tremble.

The Lord of hosts is with us:
the God of Jacob is our stronghold.

Come then and see what the Lord has done:
what destruction he has brought upon the earth.

He makes wars to cease in all the world:
he breaks the bow and shatters the spear,
and burns the chariots in the fire.

'Be still and know that I am God:
I will be exalted among the nations,
I will be exalted upon the earth.'

The Lord of hosts is with us:
the God of Jacob is our stronghold.

Verses from PSALM 91

He who dwells in the shelter of the Most High:
who abides under the shadow of the Almighty,

he will say to the Lord,
'You are my refuge and my stronghold:
my God in whom I trust.'

For he will deliver you from the snare of the hunter:
and from the destroying curse.

He will cover you with his wings,
and you will be safe under his feathers:
his faithfulness will be your shield and defence.

You shall not be afraid of any terror by night:
or of the arrow that flies by day,

of the pestilence that walks about in darkness:
or the plague that destroys at noonday.

For he will command his angels:
to keep you in all your ways.

They will bear you up in their hands:
lest you dash your foot against a stone.

PSALM 121

I lift up my eyes to the hills:
   but where shall I find help?

My help comes from the Lord:
   who has made heaven and earth.

He will not suffer your foot to stumble:
   and he who watches over you will not sleep.

Be sure he who has charge of Israel:
   will neither slumber nor sleep.

The Lord himself is your keeper:
   the Lord is your defence upon your right hand;

the sun shall not strike you by day:
   nor shall the moon by night.

The Lord will defend you from all evil:
   it is he who will guard your life.

The Lord will defend your going out and your coming in:
   from this time forward for evermore.

Verses from PSALM 145

The Lord upholds all those who stumble:
   and raises up those that are bowed down.

The eyes of all look to you in hope:
   and you give them their food in due season;

you open wide your hand:
   and fill all things living with your bounteous gift.

The Lord is just in all his ways:
   and faithful in all his dealings.

The Lord is near to all who call upon him:
   to all who call upon him in truth.

He will fulfil the desire of those that fear him:
   he will hear their cry, and save them.

My mouth shall speak the praises of the Lord:
   and let all flesh bless his holy name,
   for ever and ever.

OLD TESTAMENT READINGS

Isaiah 35.3-6 (RSV)

Strengthen the weak hands,
and make firm the feeble knees.
Say to those who are of a fearful heart,
'Be strong, fear not!
Behold, your God
will come with vengeance,
with the recompense of God.
He will come and save you.'

Then the eyes of the blind shall be opened,
and the ears of the deaf unstopped;
then shall the lame man leap like a hart,
and the tongue of the dumb sing for joy.
For waters shall break forth in the wilderness,
and streams in the desert.

Isaiah 40.27-31 (RSV)

Why do you say, O Jacob,
and speak, O Israel,
'My way is hid from the Lord,
and my right is disregarded by my God'?
Have you not known? Have you not heard?
The Lord is the everlasting God,
the Creator of the ends of the earth.
He does not faint or grow weary,
his understanding is unsearchable.
He gives power to the faint,
and to him who has no might he increases strength.
Even youths shall faint and be weary,
and young men shall fall exhausted;
but they who wait for the Lord shall renew their strength,
they shall mount up with wings like eagles,
they shall run and not be weary,
they shall walk and not faint.

Isaiah 53.3-5 (RSV)

He was despised and rejected by men;
  a man of sorrows, and acquainted with grief;
and as one from whom men hide their faces
  he was despised, and we esteemed him not.

Surely he has borne our griefs
  and carried our sorrows;
yet we esteemed him stricken,
  smitten by God, and afflicted.

But he was wounded for our transgressions,
  he was bruised for our iniquities;
upon him was the chastisement that made us whole,
  and with his stripes we are healed.

NEW TESTAMENT READINGS

Romans 8.31b-end (RSV)

If God is for us, who is against us? He who did not spare his own Son but gave him up for us all, will he not also give us all things with him? Who shall bring any charge against God's elect? It is God who justifies; who is to condemn? Is it Christ Jesus, who died, yes, who was raised from the dead, who is at the right hand of God, who indeed intercedes for us? Who shall separate us from the love of Christ? Shall tribulation, or distress, or persecution, or famine, or nakedness, or peril, or sword? As it is written:

'For thy sake we are being killed all the day long;
we are regarded as sheep to be slaughtered.'

No, in all these things we are more than conquerors through him who loved us. For I am sure that neither death, nor life, nor angels, nor principalities, nor things present, nor things to come, nor powers, nor height, nor depth, nor anything else in all creation, will be able to separate us from the love of God in Christ Jesus our Lord.

2 Corinthians 1.3-5 (NEB)

Praise be to the God and Father of our Lord Jesus Christ, the all-merciful Father, the God whose consolation never fails us! He comforts us in all our troubles, so that we in turn may be able to comfort others in any trouble of theirs and to share with them the consolation we ourselves receive from God. As Christ's cup of suffering overflows, and we suffer with him, so also through Christ our consolation overflows.

2 Corinthians 12.7-10 (RSV)

And to keep me from being too elated by the abundance of revelations, a thorn was given me in the flesh, a messenger of Satan, to harass me, to keep me from being too elated. Three times I besought the Lord about this, that it should leave me; but he said to me, 'My grace is sufficient for you, for my power is made perfect in weakness.' I will all the more gladly boast of my weaknesses, that the power of Christ may rest upon me. For the sake of Christ, then, I am content with weaknesses, insults, hardships, persecutions, and calamities; for when I am weak, then I am strong.

Ephesians 3.14-21 (RSV)

I bow my knees before the Father, from whom every family in heaven and on earth is named, that according to the riches of his glory he may grant you to be strengthened with might through his Spirit in the inner man, and that Christ may dwell in your hearts through faith; that you, being rooted and grounded in love, may have power to comprehend with all the saints what is the breadth and length and height and depth, and to know the love of Christ which surpasses knowledge, that you may be filled with all the fullness of God.

Now to him who by the power at work within us is able to do far more abundantly than all that we ask or think, to him be glory in the church and in Christ Jesus to all generations, for ever and ever. Amen.

Philippians 1.20-26 (JB)

My one hope and trust is that I shall never have to admit defeat, but that now as always I shall have the courage for Christ to be glorified in my body, whether by my life or by my death. Life to me, of course, is Christ, but then death would bring me something more; but then again, if living in this body means doing work which is having good results — I do not know what I should choose. I am caught in this dilemma: I want to be gone and be with Christ, which would be very much the better, but for me to stay alive in this body is a more urgent need for your sake. This weighs with me so much that I feel sure I shall survive and stay with you all, and help you to progress in the faith and even increase your joy in it; and so you will have another reason to give praise to Christ Jesus on my account when I am with you again.

Philippians 4.4-7 (RSV)

Rejoice in the Lord always; again I will say, Rejoice. Let all men know your forbearance. The Lord is at hand. Have no anxiety about anything, but in everything by prayer and supplication with thanksgiving let your requests be made known to God. And the peace of God, which passes all understanding, will keep your hearts and your minds in Christ Jesus.

James 5.14, 15 (RSV)

Is any among you sick? Let him call for the elders of the church, and let them pray over him, anointing him with oil in the name of the Lord; and the prayer of faith will save the sick man, and the Lord will raise him up; and if he has committed sins, he will be forgiven.

GOSPELS

Matthew 8.5-13 (JB)

When Jesus went into Capernaum a centurion came up and pleaded with him. 'Sir,' he said, 'my servant is lying at home paralysed, and in great pain.' 'I will come myself and cure him,' said Jesus. The centurion replied, 'Sir, I am not worthy to have you under my roof; just give the word and my servant will be cured. For I am under authority myself, and have soldiers under me; and I say to one man: Go, and he goes; to another: Come here, and he comes; to my servant: Do this, and he does it.' When Jesus heard this he was astonished and said to those following him, 'I tell you solemnly, nowhere in Israel have I found faith like this. And I tell you that many will come from east and west to take their places with Abraham and Isaac and Jacob at the feast in the kingdom of heaven; but the subjects of the kingdom will be turned out into the dark, where there will be weeping and grinding of teeth.' And to the centurion Jesus said, 'Go back, then; you have believed, so let this be done for you.' And the servant was cured at that moment.

Matthew 8.14-17 (JB)

Going into Peter's house Jesus found Peter's mother-in-law in bed with fever. He touched her hand and the fever left her, and she got up and began to wait on him. That evening they brought him many who were possessed by devils. He cast out the spirits with a word and cured all who were sick. This was to fulfil the prophecy of Isaiah: He took our sicknesses away and carried our diseases for us.

Mark 2.1-12 (NEB)

When Jesus returned to Capernaum, the news went round that he was at home; and such a crowd collected that the space in front of the door was not big enough to hold them. And while he was proclaiming the message to them, a man was brought who was paralysed. Four men were carrying him, but because of the crowd they could not get him near. So they opened up the roof over the place where Jesus was, and when they had broken through they lowered the stretcher on which the paralysed man was lying. When Jesus saw their faith, he said to the paralysed man, 'My son, your sins are forgiven.'

Now there were some lawyers sitting there and they thought to themselves, 'Why does the fellow talk like that? This is blasphemy! Who but God alone can forgive sins?' Jesus knew in his own mind that this was what they were thinking, and said to them: 'Why do you harbour thoughts like these? Is it easier to say to this paralysed man, "Your sins are forgiven", or to say, "Stand up, take your bed, and walk"? But to convince you that the Son of Man has the right on earth to forgive sins' — he turned to the paralysed man — 'I say to you, stand up, take your bed, and go home.' And he got up, and at once took his stretcher and went out in full view of them all, so that they were astounded and praised God. 'Never before', they said, 'have we seen the like.'

Luke 11.9-13 (JB)
Jesus said, 'I say to you: Ask, and it will be given to you; search, and you will find; knock, and the door will be opened to you. For the one who asks always receives; the one who searches always finds; the one who knocks will always have the door opened to him. What father among you would hand his son a stone when he asked for bread? Or hand him a snake instead of a fish? Or hand him a scorpion if he asked for an egg? If you then, who are evil, know how to give your children what is good, how much more will the heavenly Father give the Holy Spirit to those who ask him!'

Luke 17.11-19 (JB)
Now on the way to Jerusalem Jesus travelled along the border between Samaria and Galilee. As he entered one of the villages, ten lepers came to meet him. They stood some way off and called to him, 'Jesus! Master! Take pity on us.' When he saw them he said, 'Go and show yourselves to the priests'. Now as they were

going away they were cleansed. Finding himself cured, one of them turned back praising God at the top of his voice and threw himself at the feet of Jesus and thanked him. The man was a Samaritan. This made Jesus say, 'Were not all ten made clean? The other nine, where are they? It seems that no one has come back to give praise to God, except this foreigner.' And he said to the man, 'Stand up and go on your way. Your faith has saved you.'

John 6.47-51 (JB)

Jesus said:
'I tell you most solemnly,
everybody who believes has eternal life.
I am the bread of life.
Your fathers ate the manna in the desert
and they are dead;
but this is the bread that comes down from heaven,
so that a man may eat it and not die.
I am the living bread which has come down from heaven.
Anyone who eats this bread will live for ever;
and the bread that I shall give
is my flesh, for the life of the world.'

John 9.1-7 (NEB)

As he went on his way Jesus saw a man blind from his birth. His disciples put the question, 'Rabbi, who sinned, this man or his parents? Why was he born blind?' 'It is not that this man or his parents sinned,' Jesus answered; 'he was born blind so that God's power might be displayed in curing him. While daylight lasts we must carry on the work of him who sent me; night comes, when no one can work. While I am in the world I am the light of the world.'

With these words he spat on the ground and made a paste with the spittle; he spread it on the man's eyes, and said to him, 'Go and wash in the pool of Siloam.' (The name means 'sent'.) The man went away and washed, and when he returned he could see.

John 10.14, 15, 27-30 (JB)

Jesus said:
'I am the good shepherd;
I know my own
and my own know me,
just as the Father knows me
and I know the Father;
and I lay down my life for my sheep.
The sheep that belong to me listen to my voice;
I know them and they follow me.
I give them eternal life;
they will never be lost
and no one will ever steal them from me.
The Father who gave them to me is greater than anyone,
and no one can steal from the Father.
The Father and I are one.'

John 14.1-3, 27 (JB)

Jesus said:
'Do not let your hearts be troubled.
Trust in God still, and trust in me.
There are many rooms in my Father's house;
if there were not, I should have told you.
I am going now to prepare a place for you,
and after I have gone and prepared you a place,
I shall return to take you with me;
so that where I am
you may be too.

Peace I bequeath to you,
my own peace I give you,
a peace the world cannot give, this is my gift to you.
Do not let your hearts be troubled or afraid.'

AUTHORIZATION

The Services in *Ministry to the Sick* are authorized pursuant to Canon B2 of the Canons of the Church of England for use from 1 June 1983 until 31 December 1990.

The versions of the Psalter which have been authorized for use by the General Synod under Canons B1 and B2 are the Prayer Book Psalter, the Revised Psalter, and the Liturgical Psalter.

COPYRIGHT

Reproduction for a Single Occasion A service or combination of services provided for in *Ministry to the Sick* may be reproduced for use on a single occasion without written permission of the Central Board of Finance and without payment of a fee provided that the copies are not sold, that the name of the parish, cathedral or institution is shown on the front cover or front page with the date and description of the service, and that the following acknowledgement is included:

> *Ministry to the Sick*, material from which is included in this service, is copyright © The Central Board of Finance of the Church of England 1983.

Copyright in biblical passages and psalms is vested in the various holders (see Acknowledgements); but no application needs to be made for permission to reproduce in such a service biblical passages or extracts from the Liturgical Psalter set out in the Appendix.

Parishes wishing to reproduce a service or combination of services from the book *for use on more than one occasion* must request in advance permission to do so from the Legal Adviser to the General Synod.

Requests to reproduce any portion of *Ministry to the Sick* should be addressed to:

The Legal Adviser to the General Synod,
Church House, Dean's Yard,
Westminster, London SW1P 3NZ

ACKNOWLEDGEMENTS

Biblical passages are reproduced with permission from

The Revised Standard Version of the Bible (RSV), copyright 1946, 1952, © 1971, 1973 by The Division of Christian Education of the National Council of the Churches of Christ in the USA

The New English Bible (NEB), © 1961, 1970 Oxford and Cambridge University Presses

The Jerusalem Bible (JB), © 1966 by Darton, Longman & Todd Ltd and Doubleday and Company Inc.

Psalms from the Liturgical Psalter, which is © English text 1976, 1977, David L Frost John A Emerton, Andrew A Macintosh, all rights reserved, are reproduced with permission of William Collins Sons & Co Ltd.

The Book of Common Prayer is Crown copyright; material from the Prayer Book (some in adapted form) is reproduced with permission.

A number of copyright prayers from *Prayers for Use at the Alternative Services* compiled and adapted by David Silk (Cassell/Mowbray), and the prayer 'Father, we pray for those who are mentally ill . . .' (adapted) by Timothy Dudley-Smith are reproduced with permission.

Designed by Keith Murgatroyd (Hon) MRNCM, FSIAD, PPSTD

Set in Lasercomp Palatino type at the University Press, Cambridge

Printed in Great Britain by Alden Colour

Jointly published by the following publishers of The Alternative Service Book 1980

Cambridge University Press, Trumpington Street, Cambridge CB2 1RP
William Clowes (Publishers) Ltd, Beccles, Suffolk NR34 9QE
Oxford University Press, Walton Street, Oxford OX2 6DP
SPCK, Holy Trinity Church, Marylebone Road, London NW1 4DU